CHARLIE CHAPLIN

The Silent Little Tramp

THE HISTORY HOUR

HISTORY

CONTENTS

❧ I ❧

INTRODUCTION

❧❧❧

Charlie Chaplin was one of the most versatile and flexible of all comedians and actors during the beginning of the 20th Century. While he started his career in the common genre of his times – around 1920 – he always added his own individual flair to his films. He was unafraid and experimental in his approach. Chaplin's early films followed in lock step with the slapstick approaches he learned in his vaudeville days, but introduced new themes into his work, such as those that reflected new societal directions. He even experimented with dark humor – a most unusual trend that was imitated by others. Improvisation characterized his silent work, and that tended to be a challenge to his fellow actors. Chaplin was, however, very well-liked among his colleagues as well as respected by them.

Chaplin came from a background of dire poverty, and the flavor of the common man and the plight of poor people permeated his movies, especially his trademark character, the "***Little Tramp***." That accounted for much of his popular appeal. When he was only 26-years-old, he negotiated a half-a-million-dollar contract!

Charlie Chaplin was a perfectionist. He designed every scene carefully and was willing to conduct as many as 20 retakes in order to get a scene absolutely correct. Sometimes the actors he worked were puzzled by him. One time, Marlon Brando, asked him what the character's motivation was in a few segments. Chaplin replied,

> *"Forget about motivation, just do it as I tell you to do it.*
> *That's your motivation!"*

Chaplin had a wild love life, and sometimes impregnated women whom he married out of obligation. He was a very good-looking man when young and quite charming. For him, women were easy to love. Most of the women he dated and/or married starred with him in his films and they were, as a matter of fact, quite beautiful.

The era of the Cold War between the Soviet Union that influenced the geopolitics following World War II and spilled over to the field of entertainment. At that time, Chaplin was accused of being a "**communist sympathizer**." It did appear on the surface that he had a leftist tendency, but – as he describes it – he was a "**peace-monger**." He detested war, and often looked upon it as a means to gain control of large swaths of territory at the expense of the human rights of citizens within those countries. Because of his political views, he was "**blacklisted**," and suffered a severe downturn in his career. There was a long-drawn-out investigation that followed that episode and it was intensified by J. Edgar Hoover, the U.S. attorney general during that time. Chapin was then harassed and victimized by rumors and innuendos which were rarely ever true. On one occasion, he was targeted as a potential victim of an assassination plot!

❧

His creativity was unbounded, and he wouldn't let himself be constricted by the formula-type of approach toward scriptwriting. While creative differences can sometimes destroy one's own future career, that wasn't the case with Charlie. His work blossomed under his own writing, direction and production.

❧ II ❧
FRUGAL YEARS

"A day without laughter is a day wasted."

— CHARLIE CHAPLIN

❧

Charlie Chaplin was a comic actor noted for his very unique

comedic style. Unlike dramatic actors, comedians can perform in both dramatic roles as well as comedy. Many comedic segments are based on the flip side of tragedy. Charlie Chaplin's most memorable character was "**The Little Tramp**."

৩৯৫

The opening line of Charles Dickens' novel, Tale of Two Cities, says:

"It was the best of times; it was the worst of times."

Those words describe the life of Sir Charles Chaplin. One of eleven children, he was born into poverty in Edwardian England. During that time, there was a huge gap between those who had money and those who didn't. The rich were rich, as expected, and but there was also a rise in the financial status of the middle class. The poor, on the other hand, grew poorer.

৩৯৫

Both his father and mother, Charles Sr. and Hannah, performed in music halls. She was an expert at pantomime, and it is said the Charlie learned that from her. Both of his parents felt that the boy, who was just a toddler, had talent as a performer. He participated in clog-dancing, and it was clear he had a sense of rhythm. On one occasion, his mother was sick from overwork and contracted laryngitis. One night, her laryngitis was so bad that she couldn't sing. Then Charlie – only five years old at the time – stepped in a sang a little ditty on his own. The audience loved it!

⁂

Unfortunately, Charlie Chaplin's father became a hopeless alcoholic and died at the age of 38. He had no will and, as a consequence, Hannah had virtually no income except what she could earn doing part-time nurse's work as a nurse's aide and dressmaking. Charlie tried to get small jobs – the kind of work one would let a young boy do. So, he engaged in selling flowers and washing floors. He also begged for money which he took home to his mother. Hannah was also psychologically disabled. She was committed three times to a mental institution. Then she was released twice but was committed to the institution permanently upon her third admission.

⁂

As a child, Charlie and his older half-brother, Sydney, then had to live in a workhouse. England had passed laws for the apparent protection and welfare of children. They were referred to as "*inmates*" – a term that conjures up visions of a prison. The housing was often squalid and confining. Large numbers of children were sequestered into a dormitory and required to follow strict rules. Chaplin did receive some cursory education in the rudimentary subjects but had to get out of bed at 5 am and proceed with a succession of chores after breakfast.

⁂

Any average child will break the rules, but the punishments delved out were corporal punishments and sometimes cruel. Because of the huge number of children, the caretakers often became frustrated and impatient. That gave rise to child abuse. There were laws forbidding that, but enforcement was only sporadic at best.

❧

From his childhood experiences in the theater, Charlie had a keen sense of interest in the world of acting. After his mother was released from the mental institution on her second visits, Charlie returned home. On his own, he signed up with Harry Arthur Saintsbury's operatic comedic company, Saintsbury recognized the boy's tremendous talent. He then mentored him for a number of years. Chaplin described Saintsbury as having a

"long sensitive face and an inspired forehead."

Thus, it is clear that Chaplin appreciated the important role of the visual factor in any performance.

"BILLY THE PAGEBOY"

❦

S aintsbury introduced 12-year old Charlie Chaplin to the producer, Charles Frohman, who was in the process of developing the comedic play, Sherlock Holmes. He immediately took a liking to the lad and cast him in the role of "***Billy the Pageboy***." Chaplin's first appearance in that play nearly brought the house down! Once that occurred, Frohman signed him on. There were many more performances of Sherlock Holmes following that, and that helped Frohman make the play a tremendous success. Chaplin continued with Frohman's production company for more than two years.

BURLESQUE

❦

Charlie Chaplin's brother, Sydney, also had talent in comedic acting and the two often traveled the behind-the-scenes world of the search for new and profitable work. In the late Victorian era just preceding Chaplin's birth, the art of the burlesque was popular. Burlesque is a form of parody, which satirizes serious plays. England had been inundated with the heavy works of writers like Chaucer and Shakespeare. Everyone was familiar with the characters and character-types manifest in those acts. England needed a refreshing break from having to analyze serious drama, so the exaggerated and lavish productions based on these plays was welcome. Chaplin's somber appearance against the backdrop of hilarity caused a great deal of spontaneous laughter. Strand magazine which carried a feature on the theater, often mentioned the audience's reaction to this young man, Charlie Chaplin. That, of course, opened the door for him to obtain coveted interviews with other producers.

VAUDEVILLE

✿❦✿

S oon, the burlesques style of satire morphed into performances that were not only based on satire but were comedic in and of themselves. Scriptwriters created their own plots which were light-hearted and even silly but based on the activities of daily living. Song and dance were intermingled in these acts, and Charlie had experience in both from his parents, as did his brother.

✿❦✿

Charlie Chaplin appeared as a teen in the London Coliseum, the most famous theater in England. He played in "*Jimmy the Fearless*." His brother went on to do a number of roles in his own right, but never reached the level of fame that Charlie did. Charlie and Sydney went out on tour with Fred Karno's comedy company and appeared in America as well. They achieved top billing in the theater publication, Empress. The reviewers called Charlie *"one of the best pantomime artists ever seen."*

His enactments were performed in total silence and his gyrations around the stage consisted of abrupt and staccato movements that mimicked real life as if in rapid motion. As time marched forward, Sydney became his manager and agent. His first film stint ran from 1914 to 1917.

COMPETITION AND ANTAGONISM

❧

The comedians of those times furiously competed with each other, as they do today. During his times at Vaudeville, Chaplin watched the performances of Stan Laurel and Oliver Hardy. Chaplin imitated Stan Laurel very closely. In 1910, critics accused him of plagiarizing although Laurel was never offended by that. A character that Chaplin later developed – the Lil' Tramp – appears to be nearly an exact facsimile of Laurel in terms of body positions and expressions. After Laurel was fired from his position in a music hall, the owners immediately summoned Chaplin to replace him. In 1917, when Chaplin first embarked on his film career, Laurel also arrived in New York. Chaplin was somewhat distant toward him, but later promised he would hire Laurel. He never followed through. It was conjectured that he felt threatened by Laurel's popularity. Chaplin didn't realize that a relationship with Laurel would have benefited him in the long run, as Laurel eventually ended up being heralded with the other comedy greats of the time – Harry Langdon, Buster Keaton and Harold Lloyd.

KEYSTONE STUDIO

৩৫৯

Mack Sennett, one of the owners of New York Motion Picture Company in the United States, saw Charlie Chapman's performances and thought his silent portrayals in vaudeville could attract a wider audience if they were introduced to the film industry. He had Chaplin sign a contract and had him work at Keystone Pictures studio in Los Angeles. Sennett had a lot of success with slapstick comedy and was famous for the Keystone Cops, a clumsy band of cops whose antics kept audiences entertained for years.

৩৫৯

Sennett was concerned that Chaplin, who was only 24-years-old at the time, looked too young for his parts. Chaplin himself resolved that dilemma by creating a costume composed of contradictions: coat too small, shoes too big and baggy pants that was the least stylish manner in which to dress. He had a derby with a rounded cap and sported a mustache that gave Sennett the look of age he needed. His outfit was the precursor of his most notable character, the "Little Tramp."

In 1914, Chaplin starred in a movie short called The Masquerader, in which he plays an actor who is thrown out after a poor audition. After that, Chaplin reappeared dressed up a woman and is hired on the spot. This was Chaplin's first film done in drag. Critics remarked that Charlie Chaplain made a nice-looking woman! Chaplin first met "**Fatty**" Arbuckle at Keystone. Arbuckle was already famous at the time, and mentored Chaplin in some of his future performances. Shortly after that, though, Fatty Arbuckle was accused of rape and manslaughter. Although he was cleared of the charges, he was unable to return to the same level of fame he had before.

THE "LITTLE TRAMP"

❦

round the year 1915, Chaplin developed his
trademark character, the "***Little Tramp***." He was
trying to give audiences the impression of a poor
hapless man who tried harder and harder to please. However,
the more he tried, the clumsier he seemed. Keystone let him
try out the character in Kid Auto Races at Venice (California). That movie short centered on a story about the filming
of the auto races, and Chaplin – as the tramp – kept getting in
the way of the cameraman. The humor explosively emerged
when Chaplin repeated various ways of interfering with the
"***filming***." His performance stole the stage. In time, Chaplin
perfected the character, adding some points of feigned
dignity and polite poise. He frequently improvised during the
filming, which occasionally surprised his fellow actors like
drinking soup with a cigar in his mouth! Later, they couldn't
help their responses and would even laugh during the filming.
Chaplin would often insert these ad-libs into the movies.

The movies in the early 20th Century were then all silent films. Some had musical scores in the background. This music was carefully composed and selected to deliver an emotion. Charlie started developing his own distinct character style. The films were replete with slapstick routines: butt-kicking, falling backward, somersaults, brick-throwing and neck-wringing. Chaplin developed a uniqueness in terms of his expressions which were exaggerated. For example, he would tip his derby hat at inappropriate times, stare at the sky, stick his tongue out, hit people with his cane, kick one leg in the air while running and kick people in the butt. His feet were always flayed out sideways to the point one wonders why he didn't fall down.

Chaplin managed to grab the full attention of the audience in his silent films for Keystone Pictures. With the advent of sound, the Little Tramp character could no longer come across well, because the scenes consisted of silent expressions and cock-eyed bodily movements.

Chaplin was an ambitious man and wanted his characters to receive a prominent role. He therefore had creative differences with some of the directors at Keystone Pictures like Mabel Normand in Mabel's Strange Predicament. Usually, arguments with powerful directors aren't wise in the film industry. Mack Sennett almost had to fire Chaplin for his offenses, but suddenly received numerous orders for more copies of his films, so quickly changed his mind. After clarifying Chaplin's character development, Sennett discovered that some of funniest segments of his films had been cut. Since Sennett was going to reap in more profits for him, he permitted Charlie to direct some of his own films. The first one was called Caught in the Rain. The scenario featured in that movie was about his dealings with a jealous suitor. Charlie was in the bedroom of the suitor's date and ends up stranded on her balcony in the rain trying to hide. A cop shows up and that was the opportunity for one of their trademarks "***Keystone Cop***" routines.

&

Chaplin's run with Keystone ended when Sennett refused to give him the raise he requested after his follow-up hit, Tillie's Punctured Romance.

FRUGAL TO THE POINT OF FOOLISHNESS

৩⅍৩

Having been raised in poverty, Charlie Chaplin was very money-conscious. Mack Sennett's business manager once had to ask Chaplin why he wasn't cashing all the checks he received for his salary. He responded that he didn't do that in order to prevent himself from needlessly spending money until he absolutely needed it. It was also customary, as it is today, to take turns buying everyone a round of drinks when they took a quick meal. After the other actors and crew noticed that Charlie never offered to buy a round of drinks, someone suggested that they pull names out of the hat to decide on who would pay for the last round. As a practical joke, they only put Chalie's name on all the small sheets of paper. When his name was drawn (of course), it was said that he never realized he'd been conned!

৩⅍৩

Chaplin used to rent rooms at run-down hotels and dressed

poorly. However, as he became better known, many people recognized him and pursued him for autographs. As that practice increased, Chaplin made a deal with a local restaurant to eat for free. He told the owner that his presence would draw a crowd! The man accepted his offer and he had many free meals while at Keystone.

❧

His fellow actors played another practical joke on him and rigged a toilet seat in the men's room to deliver a slight electric shock if someone used it. Although Charlie wasn't the intended target (or so they said), he used that toilet. When his companions realized that Chaplin never emerged from the bathroom, they became worried and rushed in. There was Charlie lying prone on the floor pretending he was dead!

ESSANAY FILM MANUFACTURING COMPANY

৩৩৯

Immediately after hearing that Chaplin was looking for new work, Essanay Films offered him much more than he had asked for in his culminating year at Keystone. He had not only a salary of $1250 per film but was awarded a tremendous signing bonus of $ 10,000 – a figure virtually unheard of in those days. At Essanay, he had more control over his pictures. Feeling that his earlier films only starred him, Chaplin realized that the pictures would be even more successful if he had a strong supporting cast. He hired Leo White – a German comedian who usually played an aristocratic nobleman or a slick villain – Bud Jamison – who stayed in some Chaplin roles until his singing career pulled him away from that – Ben Turpin – a noted comedian in his own right – and Edna Purviance. Chaplin discovered her at a café and fell in love with her. Purviance was actually an actress, not a comedian, but his love for this extremely attractive woman grabbed him emotionally, and he was determined to have her star in some of the pictures he made for Essanay. While at

Essanay, Chaplin had one of his two roles in drag in the movie, The Woman. It was a story about a boy who had met his lover in her house. When the girl's father came home, Charlie donned a female garb and left the house in that outfit to escape the father's wrath. That was his second role in drag.

꧁꧂

Chaplin's favorite co-star was Ben Turpin. Turpin was noted for his trademark facial expression – crossed eyes – and was an exaggerated version of an aristocrat. Like Chaplin, he added a vigorous physical style to his comedic sketches. However, unlike Chaplin, Turpin utilized spastic movements while Chaplin used more subtlety in his performances.

꧁꧂

By the year 1913, Chaplin was famous. There were Charlie Chaplin toys, cartoons, little dolls and comic strips sold all over in stores. He was only 24-years-old!

MUTUAL FILM CORPORATION

❦

I n 1916, Charlie Chaplin was recruited by Mutual. His salary was the highest in the industry – $670,000 per year. In today's dollars, that would amount to around $15 million. He was given his own studio. However, the contract he signed was extremely demanding. Chaplin had to create two-reel film every four weeks. A two-reel film ran for about 15 minutes. Using modern technology, this task would be simple. However, in the early 20th Century, stages had to be set along with all the appropriate backgrounds. Today, computer animation is very helpful, as the background scenes can be filmed separately, and some can even be done graphically, without the use of actors.

❦

One of his most famous films, The Immigrant, released in 1917, features Chaplin and his first love, Edna Purviance. Chaplin plays his role as the *"Tramp"* who is accosted by many seasick passengers and forced to dodge them during his violent vomiting episodes. After landing, he was robbed by a pickpocket, but finds a dime and invites a beautiful woman to join him for supper. Then he himself is accused of being a pickpocket. After straightening that out, he takes the woman to a restaurant and they order beans. Unfortunately, the coin falls out through a hole in his pocket. Terrified by a huge and surly waiter, he eventually manages to steal a tip from another table and used that to pay the bill. Chaplin used a coin as a prop throughout the film. Although this wouldn't meet up with today's standards for humor, it was dotted with his unique style of antics and comic gestures – characteristics that made him quite famous.

※

Chaplin was a purist who preferred to control the direction of his own films. In the past, he had creative differences with many of his supervisors. In time, Mutual imposed formulas on to the writing of the scenarios. Chaplin resented that, as it broke pace with his own style.

※

World War I occurred between the years 1914 to 1918. Many people accused Chaplin of not being patriotic and even of being downright anti-American because they thought he didn't join the military. That accusation wasn't true, as Charlie had registered for the draft after all, but was never called. Despite that, he had to defend himself frequently. Nevertheless, his films were taken abroad and shown to the Allied troops who absolutely loved them.

LOUSY DRIVER

৩৯৩

While working with the various studios, Charlie finally broke down and bought himself a car. He was a terrible driver, however. Often, he drove too slowly, and – when confronted with a predicament on the road – did odd things. Once he drove too close to a lamp post, but – half expecting himself to "***bounce***" off the post – was injured. The next mishap occurred when he saw a policeman directing traffic. Seeing the cop, he went into a panic and hit the accelerator instead of the brake. The cop was almost run over!

❦ III ❧
CREATIVITY WARS: CHAPLIN'S PRODUCTIONS PRIOR TO 1957

«Nothing is permanent in this wicked world - not even our troubles.»

Charlie Chaplin

FIRST NATIONAL PICTURES

֍

I n 1917, he parted ways amicably with Mutual. Their formulae and new rules and regulations were confining his artistic renditions, resulting in lower productivity on his part. The following years, he worked for First National and enjoyed artistic freedom for his productions. His half-brother Sydney ("**Syd**") announced to the public on his behalf,

> *"Charlie must be allowed all the time he needs and all the money for producing films the way he wants...It is quality, not quantity, we're after."*

֍

His initial movie for First National was *A Dog's Life*. It starred his girlfriend, Edna Purviance. Sydney Chaplin himself also made a cameo appearance. Edna also appeared in Chaplin's **The Pilgrim** in 1923 which shows Chaplin as an escaped convict who dons a minister's clothing and ends up in a church in rural Texas.

۞

He made a number of movies promoting the purchase of war bonds, to help finance World War I. In addition, Chaplin invested his own money to make some movies to support the purchase of war bonds. During that time, Chaplin made the risky move of producing a comedic war movie, **Shoulder Arms** and **The Bond**. The movies were smash hits.

۞

First National was reluctant to provide Chaplin with more money, as they didn't consider the investment cost-effective. The volume of production became much more important than the quality. High-quality productions are usually much more profitable, because those kinds of Chaplin movies were more memorable and long-lasting. That kind of "*tug-a-war*" approach to enterprise is very typical of the business world – even today.

۞

Charlie was anxious to find another producer to resolve that creative difference he had with them, and made some inquiries. He met the famous Douglas Fairbanks, a dashing actor and screenwriter; Mary Pickford, the beautiful actress; and D.W. Griffith, a director, writer and producer. They excited Chaplin with an idea to found their own distribution company and fund their own films. However, when the trio found out that Charlie was still obligated by contract to produce more movies for First National, they insisted he meet that obligation first.

⚜

Charlie was going through some personal traumas at that time in his life. His marriage to Mildred Harris was souring and they lost an infant son early on. Chaplin was heartbroken about that. When Mildred sued him for divorce, she tried to attach his assets. He felt confident about his upcoming movie, *The Kid*, and he had friends smuggle it into a hotel in Utah so Harris wouldn't find out about it. At the little hotel room, his friends edited it. *The Kid* was one of his most successful films. *The Kid* was a deeply personal attempt to vicariously experience life as a man born in poverty (as he was), and life as a father figure. It starred one of the most famous child actors of the early 20th Century, Jackie Coogan, and Chaplin's lover, Edna Purviance. The film is a model of the tragicomedy genre. Audiences were stunned by this unique approach and it was nearly the highest-grossing silent picture of the era. Because of its impact and quality, *The Kid* was preserved in the United States Film Registry – a great honor. Chaplin appears in his Tramp outfit for the filming of this movie.

⚜

Jackie Coogan was a virtual unknown child actor when *The Kid* was released in 1921. It was a tragicomedy – Chaplin's first attempt at that genre. It was about an adopted boy, and the setting Chaplin had designed for it resembled the attic room he and his brother lived in when they were with their mother. The dramatic part was derived from Chaplin's experiences when he was married to Mildred Harris who lost a baby during their marriage. Chaplin discovered the boy at vaudeville when he performed even as an infant. Coogan is said to have earned as much as 3 million dollars as a child actor! However, Coogan's mother, who remarried, squandered his money. With the help of a director and a lawyer, he sued. That case helped establish the California Child Actor's Bill in 1939, also called the "Coogan Act." It also led to reforms for child actors specifying work hours and education.

৩৯৫৩

His next movie, **Sunny-side**, didn't receive rave reviews, but he was emotionally drained after producing **The Kid**. In 1921, they released **The Idle Class** which utilized mistaken identities to provide humorous sequences. It also starred Edna Purviance. The "mistaken identity" theme was common to a number of Charlie Chaplin's films. Many of Chaplin's movies were short, like **Pay-Day**, **Sunny-side** and **A Day's Pleasure**. After that, Chaplin continued to work off his contract with First National Pictures.

৩৯৫৩

Once Charlie Chaplin had fulfilled his contract with First National Pictures, he was exhilarated, as he could join up with those talented people he met a year before – Fairbanks, Pickford and Griffith. Once the foursome was financing and controlling their own movies, they formed the distribution company called United Artists. This company is still in business today and gave birth to many offshoots including MGM/UA that split off to become MGM and UA (United Artists). Tom Cruise is one of its most prominent stars currently.

UNITED ARTISTS

❧

In 1922, *A Woman in Paris* was the first film Charlie released under the United Artists label. It wasn't a comedy, although there were some comedic episodes in it. Chaplin brought his sweetheart, Edna Purviance, with him to UA and she starred in the movie. Chaplin produced and directed *A Woman in Paris*, but didn't appear in the film. This was an experimental move, and the public didn't respond positively. Mary Pickford, one of his co-partners and a magnificent actress in her own right, felt differently. She said:

> *"A Woman of Paris allows us to think for ourselves and does not constantly insult your intelligence. It is a gripping human story throughout and the director (Chaplin) allows the situations to play themselves. Charlie Chaplin is a pioneer. How he knows women! I do not cry easily when seeing a picture, but after seeing Charlie's A*

> *Woman of Paris, I was all choked up – I wanted to go out to the garden and have it out by myself."*

⚜

Chaplin was very disappointed by the poor reception to *A **Woman of Paris**,* but was resilient. He recognized then that he needed to stay with comedy productions and star in his own films. To make up for the box office loss on the Paris film, he planned on producing a blockbuster film for his next project.

⚜

Chaplin did exactly that. His next film in 1925, ***The Gold Rush***, grossed over $5 million! One of the funniest scenes was of Charlie, an impoverished prospector, eating his own boot in a restaurant!

⚜

The release of his next film in 1927, ***The Circus***, starred Merna Kennedy, who was an acrobat and also a beautiful actress. Work on ***The Circus*** was sporadic, as Charlie was weathering through his painful divorce from Lita Grey at the time. ***The Circus*** did very well, but it's interesting to note that broken hearts and love affairs punctuate the plot. There were also hilarious scenes showing antics with circus monkeys to offset the seriousness of some of the segments. Chaplin had a masterful way of balancing the two themes.

A BIG RISK

৩৯৩

A fter the completion of *The Circus*, talking films were becoming very popular. Chaplin was very unfamiliar with that and missed the kind of production opportunities and the subtleties that can only be conveyed in a silent film. Therefore, his next film was silent, except for the use of a little music. Because he was taking a tremendous risk in releasing a silent movie when most were sound films, Chaplin was very neurotic over the production of his next film, *City Lights*. He became a "*madcap perfectionist*" over it, which presented a challenge for those who had to work under him. The film, *City Lights*, was released in 1931, and earned over $3 million! One astonished reviewer said:

> "Nobody in the world but Charlie Chaplin could have done
>   it. He is the only person that has that peculiar something
>   called 'audience appeal' in sufficient quality to defy the
>   popular penchant for movies that talk."

ASSASSINATION ATTEMPT!

❧

C haplin was at a turning point in his profession and the world was at a pivot point in its history. America was gradually sinking into the mud of the Great Depression, but Chaplin was experiencing a depression of his own. Now that the silent movies were anachronisms, Chaplin either had to change his whole style or retire with his own thoughts about unresolved issues in his life and career simultaneously. For a change of pace, he decided to vacation in Japan. This was an inauspicious time. World War I was over, and a treaty needed to be drawn up. It was called the Washington Naval Treaty of 1922. Its purpose was to reduce the arms buildup of the various nations who felt threatened by each other's growing power. Because this treaty was mostly Western-based, many of Japanese wanted to retain their traditional political structures and maintain their own national freedom. This treaty was incomplete, so another treaty replaced it – the London Naval Treaty of 1930.

৩৯৫৯

The caste system still dominated Japanese society in the 1930s and there was an ever-increasing envy of wealthy businessmen and the liberal political factions. In addition, the military resented the reduction of their roles within Japan. The treaties after the war had done that. Assassination plots proliferated. In 1932, the *"League of Blood Incident"* took place. It was led by a misguided monk, Nissho Inoui. This group of otherwise anonymous individuals planned to assassinate 20 people. However, they were only able to successfully eliminate Dan Takuma, the Director of the Misui Corporation and the Japanese finance minister, Junnosuke Inoue. Continuing then with his campaign, the monk, Nissho, organized a conspiracy to assassinate the Prime Minister of Japan, Inukai, and Charlie Chaplin who was going to arrive for a performance followed by a reception. By killing Chaplin, the rival faction had hoped to provoke a war with the United States – truly an unrealistic goal. The whole plan was clouded with misinformation, however, dates of Chaplin's pending arrival were confused, and Chaplin was unharmed. However, the Prime Minister Inukai was slaughtered. After that, there was supposed to be a coups d'état, but it never materialized. After the monk, Inoui, turned himself in, he wasn't imprisoned; he was celebrated as a patriot!.

৩৯৫৯

After that episode, Chaplin raced back to Los Angeles where he had been living. He underestimated the power of these political shenanigans. After returning home, Chaplin was still left to puzzle about his career.

INDUSTRIALIZATION OF THE
UNITED STATES

৩৫৩

The industrialization of America began in the late 19th Century, and grew at an exponential rate. The Great Depression severely hampered growth, but gradually the economy again picked up. Technologies were developing at the breakneck speed, as factories increased in size and number. The emphasis was upon a large cheap labor force who could run the huge machinery in the plants across the United States. Automation was introduced and every factory consisted of streamlined processes. Assembly lines existed in nearly every factory in the cities. Man and machine worked together in shifts around the clock, turning out millions of products per year. Most products were now consumer-oriented. The emphasis was now upon production, but sometimes at the expense of human values. Although people continued to work, even over time, they resented the fact that they were somehow forced to interface with this giant machine-driven culture. Wages were often insufficient and people worked long hours for less money. Those were not good times.

૱

Charlie Chaplin couldn't ignore this political and cultural milieu and used it as a background in order to appeal to the current times. He wanted to produce a new film that had a social message that still allowed for the comedic element. Comedy in that context would help lighten the psychological impact of industrial society and the Great Depression. Everyone, Chaplin felt, would relate to such a theme.

MODERN TIMES

❦

In 1936, Chaplin, still working at United Artists studios, wrote, produced and directed this timely message movie called **Modern Times**. It wasn't a silent movie this time, but had little dialogue. It was a political commentary and satire about man's struggle to survive in this machine-dominated world.

❦

The movie starred Paulette Goddard and his long-time friend, Henry Bergman. Bergman also appeared in some of Chaplin's earlier films, **The Gold Rush**, **The Circus** and **City Lights**.

❦

Modern Times pictured the industrial society most poignantly. The hero, Chaplin in his "**Tramp**" persona, was a pathetic factory worker required to screw in nuts at a steadily increasing rate in this slapstick-rigged routine. When he explodes with anxiety and provokes a one-person riot he is imprisoned. Through some wacky twisted circumstances, he becomes a hero when it looks like he stopped another prison riot. After being freed, he was then hungry and desperate.

༺༻

The scenes in that movie comically relate the psychological reaction to being controlled by a mechanically-oriented society and reflected the poverty that manifested itself during this period. In a more emotional phase of the movie, he used the story to bring forward the beauty and value of human relationships above the importance of the technology in which people are enmeshed. The movie is a message about never failing to lose what is most valuable in life.

CHAPLIN AND CHURCHILL

❀

C harlie Chaplin met Winston Churchill in England even before he was the prime minister of England. Although it wasn't that well-known at the time, Chaplin had strong political views. He and Churchill got into a lengthy discussion about the labor government – a fact which surprised Churchill. He even wanted Chaplin to play Napoleon someday. He had invited Chaplin to his country residence at Chartwell and they had a delightful dinner with other dignitaries. When the discussions meandered on to political topics with which Churchill disagreed, Churchill grew silent and looked upset. Then Charlie broke the ice by sticking two forks in a couple of bread rolls, and did a dance routine from *The Gold Rush*. Although they differed in their political views, Churchill enjoyed Chaplin's well-honed sense of humor. When a dinner conversation strayed on to world leaders, Chaplin said that the "*Gandhi's or Lenin's*" of this world were just giving voice to the "*masses*." At one point, Churchill suggested that Chaplin should run for Parliament!

Later on at the table, a guest asked Chaplin what role he would play next, and Chaplin dryly replied

"Jesus Christ."

That caught everyone off guard, but – after a moment or two of silence – Churchill then quipped,

"Have you cleared the rights?"

The whole table then burst into laughter. Both Churchill and Chaplin were quick-witted and had a fine way of converting heavy pensive discussions into humor. The art of every comedian is to make statements by exaggerating the serious to its ultimate conclusion. It was a commentary on the human condition.

SHADOWS AND SUBSTANCE

❦

I n 1944, Chaplin bought the rights to a little-known play called ***Shadow and Substance*** by Paul Carroll. It was controversial as it was critical of the Catholic Church in Ireland and the world in general. It centered upon a critique about the view that the Catholic Church had deviated from its original beliefs. In the play, a young girl practices a pure and innocent form of Catholicism while the current practice of the faith differed substantially. Although he had misgivings about O'Neill in the starring role, he decided he might give her a chance. He even had his mistress, Joan Barry, do a reading on it, and toyed with the idea of casting her instead of O'Neill. With regard to ***Shadows and Substances***, however, his partners at UA had misgivings about the religious implications of the play and he shelved it.

❦

Chaplin and O'Neill married in 1943, but then she gave up her acting career except for one performance as a stand-in for Claire Bloom in one of his last movies, ***Limelight***.

CHAPLIN GETS "BOOED" AT
MONSIEUR VERDOUX

୬୬୬

The theme of this 1947 movie was categorized as "black humor," meaning a deeply subtle reference to the idiocy of evil. The character, Monsieur Verdoux, a laid-off bank clerk, started marrying wealthy women and then murdering them for their money. Many mishaps take place, which lead to laughter. This was an era when Communism was on the horizon as a political philosophy. In this film of Chaplin's there was no overt reference to Communism or politics until near the end of the film. At the end of the movie, however, Chaplin – playing Verdoux – gives a monologue condemning the world for encouraging mass murders through wars and the use of weapons of mass destruction. Verdoux made the fateful observation, that

"...one murder makes a villain; millions a hero."

Audiences disliked the movie intensely. Likewise, it aroused the interest of the FBI director, J. Edgar Hoover who saw it as a condemnation of America. In 1945, the United States had dropped the A-Bomb over Hiroshima and Nagasaki that ended World War II in the Pacific. This film met a poor reception in America, and triggered boycotts of the movie theaters which showed it. Its reception in Europe was somewhat better, especially in France.

LIMELIGHT

※

The movie, ***Limelight***, might more aptly be named "***Twilight***," as it was one of Chaplin's last films. It was shot in London and premiered in 1953. Following Charlie Chaplin's new tragicomedy style, it was the story of a drunken "***has-been***" comedian – Calvero – who saves a dancer from committing suicide. She then makes a comeback in her career, but "**Calvero**," played by Chaplin, failed to make a comeback. The lead female part was played by Claire Bloom. Claire Bloom wasn't known at that time, and it is said that Chaplin "***discovered***" her.

※

Chaplin's son, Sydney, by his marriage with Lita Grey, had a supporting role in the movie along with the famous Buster Keaton. Chaplin knew Keaton very well, having been a fellow actor with him around 1917. Four of Chaplin's children appeared in it, although they weren't credited. This movie had a tragic ending, as Calvero dies on the sidelines. His fourth (and last) wife, Oona O'Neill, also appeared as an extra.

◈

Buster Keaton was enormously popular earlier in his career, and Chaplin had him appear in ***Limelight***, as his life was similar to the story of Calvero. Later in his career, Keaton ended up writing lines for Abbott and Costello. Keaton sadly died in poverty.

◈

In 1953, ***Limelight*** premiered in Europe, but was boycotted in the United States due to McCarthyism, which was a campaign against those accused of being Communist sympathizers. Chaplin had been caught in that dragnet and his reputation was all but ruined.

FOOTLIGHTS, A NOVELLA

❧

Footlights was the one and only written fictional piece that Charlie Chaplin wrote. The manuscript was pieced together from scraps of notes Chaplin had written, and it was considered autobiographical. It was published in Brazil in 2014, but written much sooner. The backdrop for **Footlights** was like that of **Limelight**, but had parts in it that reflected Chaplin's innermost thoughts and feelings. Much of it was written in 1948 when the FBI was investigating him.

❧

Footlights is the story of a comedian whose career has taken a downturn. It mirrors Chaplin's character, "**Calvero**," whom Chaplin projected was at the end of his career. In the book, it portrays Calvero as the sad clown beaten down by life.

CHARLIE CHAPLIN'S MUSIC

❀

Once "***talkies***" were introduced into the theater, Chaplin exercised his musical talents. He hadn't studied music formally, but had an excellent ear. His scores were used in many of his productions, such as ***Modern Times***, ***Monsieur Verdoux*** and ***The Great Dictator***. Chaplin himself tinkered with a cello and a violin he had bought used, and the sound of his musical practice at night bothered his neighbors. He also plunked away at the piano. In time, even the neighbors began to enjoy it, as it was a curious admixture of brass and clarinets.

❀

By 1931, when Chaplin wrote and directed his film ***City Lights***, the "***talkies***" were in style. Chaplin did release that as a talkie. However, taking advantage of the addition of musical scores to movies, he composed an entire medley of musical scores for the background. He used music to created moods for the different settings in the segments that composed the film. Later on, he added his own musical scores to his former movies that were produced during the era of the silent films.

❧ IV ❧
SCANDALOUS LOVE LIFE

"To truly laugh, you must be able to take your pain, and play with it!"

— CHARLIE CHAPLIN

EDNA PURVIANCE

꧁꧂

Edna Purviance was Charlie Chaplin's first relationship. He had starred with her in his early career, and it was said that, through her influence, his style warmed up from its initial rough-and-tumble mentality. Purviance was a gentle soul. After Chaplin left Essanay Studio, though, their relationship faded. Purviance came from a strong familial and religious background, and was desirous of returning home to Nevada, her home state. Chaplin was immersed in the hectic pace of New York City and they decided to part ways. Edna was intelligent and self-sufficient, and proceeded to develop her own career independently.

POLA NEGRI

🙰

C harlie Chaplin met a German-speaking Polish girl, Pola Negri, in Hollywood during the 1920s. She deliberately tried to seduce him at the Hollywood affair, and was successful. They got engaged. Negri was already a success in the movies at the time and called a *"femme fatale"* or a *"vamp."* Negri herself said that Chaplin fell madly in love with her but was an "inept" lover and they had a stormy relationship. Despite that, Negri took a fervent interest in him, but she had very expensive tastes. Chaplin hadn't quite made it to the top of his success and they split up because Charlie knew he couldn't afford her.

MILDRED HARRIS

☙❧

Mildred Harris was a child star since about the age of ten. At age sixteen, she made it her business to meet the famous Charlie Chaplin. Harris was strikingly beautiful and started dating Charlie. One day, she announced she was pregnant and they married quickly, as it was unacceptable to have children outside of wedlock. As it turned out, she wasn't pregnant. It's unknown to this day as to whether or not it was a false pregnancy, or a fabrication concocted by Harris. Like Chaplin, Mildred was ambitious and did receive a couple of film contracts based upon her relationship with Chaplin. She did become pregnant a year later, but the child died within three days of his birth. Occasionally, when two actors marry, jealousy between the two can occur and it did in this case. Chaplin wondered about the movie offers she received, questioning whether she showed real talent or not. This was Charlie Chaplin's first marriage and he had difficulty adjusting to married life. That significantly slowed him down in terms of his speed of production, and he was criticized because of that. After Mildred developed a drinking problem, their marriage became toxic and they divorced in 1944.

LILLITA "LITA" MCMURRAY GREY

❦

Coincidentally, Mildred Harris and Lillita Grey met each other during Chaplin's filming of The Kid. Chaplin had a relationship with Lillita, also known as "*Lita*," when she was just 16-years-old. When she became pregnant, Chaplin hid her at the home of a trusted friend and tried to insist that she have an abortion. Abortion was illegal at the time, but Chaplin had access to enough money to have it performed without deleterious medical results. She refused, so he reluctantly married her shortly thereafter in 1924, and revealed the birth of a child after that – Charlie Spencer Chaplin, Jr. He wanted it to appear as if she gave birth after, not before, the marriage. Lita then had another male child a year later – Sydney Chaplin, named after Charlie's half-brother. The marriage was founded on rocky ground from the start and doomed to failure. Chaplin even grew suspicious of her and felt that she had married him only for his money. He once compared their marriage as being only a little bit better than being in prison. Reportedly, Chaplin had a number of love affairs outside the marriage.

◌⁜◌

Lita was very unhappy in the relationship as well and sued for divorce. As soon as he discovered her intention to divorce him, Chaplin tried to hide his assets from her, afraid that he would lose too much money in a divorce. She signed a court order demanding him to cease and desist from doing that. Lita's lawyers, in order to win a larger settlement for her, attempted to ruin Chaplin's reputation. The 1924 divorce filing was 52 pages long! He was ordered by the court to pay millions of dollars. The money was put in trust for the children.

◌⁜◌

This scandal hit all the Hollywood and national newspapers at the time. It set the trend for the gossip columns and social media of today. Chaplin himself attempted to keep his young sons from the discomfort of the scandal from his two sons – Charlie Chaplin, Jr and Sydney Chaplin. Both of them were in Chaplin's last film, Limelight.

PAULETTE GODDARD

❦

Paulette had a budding career when she met Charlie Chaplin at a party. She was a fashion model as a child and appeared as an extra in a couple of films. Then she played in Ziegfeld's musicals and even performed with Laurel and Hardy two times – once in 1929 and again in 1932. Then she was luckily hired by Sam Goldwyn, a major film producer. She appeared in eight movies for him. Goddard also did a couple of movies for Hal Roach Studios.

❦

Chaplin met her during her stint with Goldwyn and it was a whirlwind romance. By this time – 1936 – Charlie had more time to himself. He invited Goddard to a few social occasions and liked her style tremendously. She had also been working for MGM, the sister company of United Artists. However, she didn't relate well to Samuel Goldwyn, so – when Charlie offered her a role in his upcoming movie, Modern Times, she seized upon the opportunity. The two of them visited China and reportedly they were married in Canton. Both Goddard and Chaplin were obsessed with their careers. In 1936, their careers veered in different directions. After repeated attempts at reconciliation, the two grew far apart emotionally and seldom saw each other. They divorced in 1942.

JOAN BARRY

☙

While he was married to Paulette Goddard, Chaplin had a love affair with Joan Barry in 1941. Goddard and Chaplin were leading nearly separate lives at that time which was toward the end of their marriage. Chaplin liked her at her audition, saying, she had

"a talent as great as any I've seen in my whole life."

☙

During Barry and Chaplin's love affair, Barry volitionally terminated two pregnancies. After those, Joan then gave birth to a girl by the name of Carol Ann in 1943. Their relationship terminated when Joan Barry started to show schizophrenic behaviors and embarrassed him on a number of occasions. She started drinking to excess, would come home at all hours of the night, and once threatened him with a gun. Chaplin married to Oona O'Neill at that time (see below), but Joan filed a paternity suit. Chaplin went for tests which showed he wasn't the father. However, Barry's attorney had that evidence declared inadmissible because of Chaplin, or so it was rumored, had the blood tests falsified! The Court then ordered that Chaplin must pay child support. He did that until Carol was 21-years-old, as per the court ruling. Eventually, Joan Barry was committed to a state mental institution.

❦

His relationship with Barry contributed to part of an investigation commanded by J. Edgar Hoover during the mid-1940s. The USA at that time was conducting a rather paranoid hunt for those whom they suspected of being communistic. Chaplin got caught up in that dragnet and charged with a number of offenses, including a violation of the Mann Act. The Mann Act forbade transporting a woman across a state border for the purposes of having sexual intercourse. That was a rather far-fetched accusation, and Chaplin was acquitted, however.

OONA MCNEILL

❦

Oona O'Neill was the daughter of Eugene O'Neill, the famous Irish playwright. She was a socialite who was often seen in the company of Gloria Vanderbilt and other Hollywood notables. In the early 1940s, she considered a career in acting. She only got a few roles in local theater in New Jersey where she came from. Her film agent then introduced her to Charlie Chaplin, who was immediately taken with her. However, she was still very young – just 17-years-old. Before he could rewrite and produce his next play, however, Chaplin fell in love with her. They eloped and married in 1943. Charlie described their meeting as the "*happiest event of his life*." Sadly, her father disowned her upon learning of the marriage. Eugene O'Neill and Chaplin were both the same age. O'Neill did relent in his negativity toward Chaplain when one of the last films, Lime-light, was finally shown in the United States.

❦

After her marriage, Oona gave up her career as an actress. They first lived in London. Entertainers were harassed in the U.S. for suspected Communist activities. Oona and Charlie finally settled in Switzerland. They had eight children.

V

THE EPITOME OF
CHAPLIN'S POLITICAL
SATIRE

"Life could be wonderful if people would leave you alone."

— CHARLIE CHAPLIN

❦

The assassination attempt on Charlie Chaplin in 1932 and the economic conditions of the United States after the Great Depression, awoke two personality reactions in him. The Great Depression served to bitterly remind him of his poverty as a child. In addition, the changes required in his industry, basically that of the transition from silent movies into films with sound, were both traumatic to him. His love life also had its pitfalls and failures. It seemed to him that he had been thrown into a turbulent world. He couldn't rely on his tried and traditional art forms any longer. Not only his art, but his life had changed.

❧

Feeling an urgent need to relate to his audience and leave a legacy that wasn't merely filled with slapstick silence, he wanted to make a political statement through the vehicle of his work.

❧

The year was now 1939. Europe had just emerged from the ravages of World War I. Germany, in particular, was still embittered by the peace treaty, The Treaty of Versailles of 1919 which ended that war. It was overloaded with debt and forced to surrender territory. Germany wanted to revise the Treaty in the 1920s and 1930s. Instability both economic and political was widespread throughout Europe, and – to some extent – America. In Europe, there was an outcry for a return to totalitarian rule. People grew weary of political factions within their countries still vying for power while the population suffered from economic downturns.

❧

Adolph Hitler inspired his people to feel proud of themselves and their heritage after the devastation of their country. Germany was practically in ruins. Once he became Chancellor of Germany, he called his movement Nazism. Hitler promised economic recovery and a patriotic return to nationalism. However, he severely repressed any dissension. After a while, fear reigned among its citizens. Those who were loyal to Hitler were rewarded but were sometimes required to do cruel deeds. Benito Mussolini of Italy was of the same ilk. His movement was slightly different, but similar. It was called Fascism. Both of those countries pursued expansionist policies and wanted to overrun Europe in order to create "*little empires*" of their own.

৩৩৩

Other countries in the modern world vehemently opposed Hitler in particular but were reluctant to go to war due to their own economic crises. In 1939, after Germany invaded Poland, Europe exploded into World War II.

৩৩৩

Everyone learned about Hitler. His propaganda films appeared across the movie screens. People of the many nations became familiar with his style and mannerisms.

THE MAKING OF CHARLIE
CHAPLIN'S THE GREAT
DICTATOR

※

Like his movie, Modern Times, Chaplin envisioned making a politically-charged satire, but wanted to pepper it with humor. As he looked upon the face of Hitler with his stubby mustache, Charlie Chaplin saw a resemblance between that and his own mustache. Chaplin felt that Hitler and his reign of terror deserved ridicule. Hitler, of course, was controversial to use as a character, but Chaplin's movie, The Great Dictator, wasn't the first movie to do that. It was preceded by "***You Nazly Spy***!" which the Three Stooges released, and the "***Testament of Dr. Mabuse***" by Fritz Lang.

※

In Chaplin's version, Hitler's name was changed to the amusing moniker, "***Adenoid Hynkel***," and Mussolini's name was altered to be "***Benzino Napaloni***," an imitation of the name, "***Napoleon***." Chaplin had his girlfriend (later his wife),

Paulette Goddard, play in the secondary role. The Jewish ghetto was the setting used in much of the film where the action took place. It played off an identity switch between Hynkel and a Jewish barber. In a mock of a Hitler speech, the master comedian, Charlie Chaplin, rattled off make-believe German, which was actually meaningless gibberish and made the audiences roar in laughter.

※

The Jewish barber ("**Schultz**" or Charlie Chaplin) then impersonated Hynkel and presents an impassioned plea, which lies totally opposite to Hitler's true views. Toward the end of the movie, the Jewish barber (Chaplin) abandoned his barber persona, turned toward the audience face-forward and passionately addressed the audience:

> *"You, the people, have the power to make this life free and*
> *beautiful, to make this life a wonderful adventure.*
> *Then – in the name of democracy – let us use that power – let*
> *us all unite. Let us fight for a new world – a decent world*
> *that will give men a chance to work – that will give*
> *youth a future and old age a security. By the promise of*
> *these things, brutes have risen to power. But they lie! They*
> *do not fulfill that promise. They never will!"*

Unlike many of his other films, Chaplin took less than a year to pull this movie together. Britain didn't release the film in its theaters right away, though, as they were going through a period in which they felt that appeasement would be the best way to handle Hitler. In 1941, they reversed that policy and welcomed any kind of negative propaganda against Germany, so it was released in England. The United States viewed it as soon as it was released, and as many as 9 million people saw it in the theaters. France didn't show the film until 1945 – after the war – but it attracted 8 million viewers.

꧁꧂

Oddly enough, the United States opened up an investigation into Chaplin and his work. Like Great Britain, America felt that The Great Dictator would influence the public into involving the United States in a war. At that time, the United States wanted to avoid war. His political views during the years of 1939 and 1940 erupted in a backlash by the American right.

꧁꧂

Jeffrey Vance, an archivist for MGM/UA became acquainted with the film in his position. He later became a noted film historian. Of "***The Great Dictator***," he said it was

"a masterful integration of comedy, politics and satire."

The Great Dictator received five nominations for the Academy Awards. The Library of Congress also chose it to be permanently preserved for being "**culturally and aesthetically significant**."

PLAGIARISM LAWSUIT

෴

C harlie Chaplin had a long-time friend, Konrad
Bercovici, who was also a screenwriter. In the 1930s,
Bercovici had suggested to Chaplin that he produce
a screenplay Bercovici wrote called "*The Two Dictators*,"
and reportedly showed him the script. Chaplin rejected it at
that time. However, when The Great Dictator was released,
Bercovici believed he saw a similarity between the two
scripts. He charged Chaplin with plagiarism and took the
case to court, claiming that the two of them had a contract
and Chaplin agreed to produce this play for him in a movie
form. On the stand, Chaplin denied that. As a matter of fact,
no written contract was ever shown in evidence. The similarity between the scripts, though, couldn't be entirely
denied. It became a matter of the word of Chaplin against
the word of Bercovici. Occasionally, an artist or writer can
glean an idea from another, and not recall from whence they
got the idea. So, most assume that the idea was of their own

making. Judge Rifkind, seeing that this case could drag out for years, suggested that Chaplin and Bercovici resolve it out of court. As it was a settlement, there was no verdict, but Chaplin paid Bercovici $ 95,000 to close the case.

GERMAN REACTION TO THE GREAT DICTATOR

❦

I t was reported that Hitler watched The Great Dictator, but his reactions are only the subject of conjecture. Nevertheless, as a retaliation, the Nazi's released a propaganda piece called The Jews Are Watching You, by Dr. Johann von Leers. Van Leers was one of the most vicious anti-Semites in Europe at the time. In this book, the writer attempted to present to the German people the contention that the Jews were plotting against them to take over the world, and that book, The Jews Are Watching You, had a long list of names of public figures who were apparently leading the movement, including Charlie Chaplin whom they called a "*Jewish acrobat*." The Nazi's had assumed for some reason that Chaplin was Jewish. (He wasn't.) That idea persisted, and rumors erupted during the filming of the movie, Limelight.

A KING OF NEW YORK DURING
THE COLD WAR

❦

During the Cold War (1947-1991), Chaplin had been blacklisted as a Communist sympathizer when this movie was released in 1957, and it had a political impact. Because of what he considered insulting behavior from the United States, he delivered a political message very directly in this film. It was a satire on McCarthyism. His ten-year-old son, Michael, co-starred with him. The purpose of the plot was to show the ridiculous behavior of the House of Un-American Activities in the U.S. Senate. The main character, "*King Shadov*" is suspected of being a Communist. In one hilarious segment, the entire House Committee on Un-American Activities is victimized by an out-of-control fire hose! Chaplin also used this film to satirize celebrities, rock n' roll music, plastic surgery, wide-screen cinema, film producers and commercialism. One segment had New York as the setting, and that was filmed at Shepperton Studios in London. He was so angry at his American rejection, that he formed a new studio called Attica Film Company to prevent it from being shown in the United States. His partnership in United Artists was threatened by that move. A King of New York made very little profit when it was released in Paris. Chaplin also denied American journalists' permission to review the film. In 1973, it was re-released after the McCarthy era was over.

MEETINGS WITH COMMUNISTS

❧

In 1954, Charlie Chaplin lunched with Zhou Enlai, the premier of the People's Republic of China and later its prime minister. Enlai wanted to publicly demonstrate that he was urbane and cultured. Chaplin also met with Nikita Khrushchev, the premier of the Soviet Union. Khrushchev wanted to show his support for the performing arts, so he was delighted to meet with Chaplin.

❧

The World Peace Prize was awarded annually by the World Peace Council, a non-governmental organization (NGO) to countries or individuals for their contribution to peace in the world. Most of the leaders of that NGO during the 1950s were communists or leftists. In 1957, Chaplin was awarded the World Peace Prize. That occurred mostly because he was willing to reach out to Zhou Enlai and Khrushchev. When the World Peace Council failed to condemn the Soviet Union for their vicious suppression of Hungary just the year before, the organization started losing popularity.

A COUNTESS FROM HONG KONG

❦

Again, Charlie Chaplin used a political theme for his film, A Countess from Hong Kong, but the reference was only a very mild one. A Countess from Hong Kong was shown in 1967 and its setting was from the World War I era during the Russian Revolution. The main actress was Sophie Loren and Marlon Brando was the co-star. Chaplin himself only made a cameo appearance as a seasick steward. Characters were exiled Russian aristocrats who were forced to live in poverty in Shanghai and Hong Kong. Many critics panned it, and it did very poorly. However, the theme music was This Is My Song, which did become a tremendous hit. The tune was extremely popular in Europe as well as the U.S. Jack Nicholson, the famous American actor, loved the movie itself and it had a cult following.

VI

CHAPLIN: A COMMUNIST? OR A GENTLEMAN FARMER?

"Life is a tragedy when seen in close-up, but a comedy in long-shot."

— CHARLIE CHAPLIN

☙❧

In 1947, America was in the throes of what was called the "***Red Scare***." It was a rather paranoid "***witch hunt***" for anyone who could possibly have had or have Communistic leanings. The came up as a result of the Cold War, a bloodless battle between America and the Soviet Union. Americans became suspicious of anyone who made comments or displayed behavior that could possibly be construed as "*anti-American*," or as favoring the totalitarian regime of the Soviet Union under Nikita Khrushchev. Harry S. Truman, the U.S. President at the time, passed an executive order to screen all federal employees first. Then he and the administration under the vitriolic leadership of Joseph McCarthy, Senator from Wisconsin, targeted anyone from the entertainment industry and financial institutions. Ads saying

"You can drive the Reds out of television, radio and Hollywood"

were circulated everywhere. That included Charlie Chaplin.

❦

In the House of Representatives, the "*House Committee on Un-American Activities*" (HUAC) was established to direct attention to any individuals in those industries including the film industry who were suspected of subversive activities.

❦

Because of Chaplin's statements at the end of his movie titled Monsieur Verdoux, he aroused the interest of J. Edgar Hoover. Chaplin's studio issued what was called the Waldorf Statement, saying that they have no communist nor left-leaning person hired, regardless of whether he or she was on staff or employed as an actor or screenwriter.

HEDDA HOPPER'S POISON PEN

૭ૐ૭

H edda Hopper started out in Hollywood as an
actress and singer. She was successful in silent
films. In the 1930s, though, her career started to go
downhill. She had a penchant for writing and knew many of
the Hollywood stars. Because of her knowledge and contacts,
she started writing a column called "*Hedda Hopper's Hollywood*." Hopper was a stern conservative in terms of politics,
and the Nazi's even ridiculed her, mocking her flamboyant
hats – which served as her trademark. She loved to spread
rumors about the love lives of actors and actresses like Joseph
Cotton and Deanna Durbin. Even producers and directors
paid attention to Hopper's opinions, and it was said that she
was instrumental in getting an Oscar awarded to Joan
Crawford.

૭ૐ૭

Hedda Hopper disliked Chaplin's political views intensely and never missed an opportunity to discredit him. The Blacklists arose around this time, and Hopper drew attention to Chaplin's apparent leftist leanings. Hopper also pointed out Chaplin's love affairs. She also helped Joan Barry out when the woman was in the initial process of suing Chaplin about the questioned paternity of Carol Ann, her child. She also criticized Chaplin for not applying for U.S. citizenship. Her continual written harassment of him was one factor leading to his being blacklisted.

BLACKLISTS

৩ﷻৡ

One of the greatest vulnerabilities to this governmental oversight was the nationality of individuals. Charlie Chaplin was born in England and came here on a VISA in 1913. The VISA ran out, but he didn't bother renewing it. Because Chaplin was so popular in the United States, the immigration authorities didn't bother to enforce the laws.

৩ﷻৡ

After World War II, Chaplin became involved in promoting the cause of peace between the United States and the Soviet Union. He called himself a "*peace-monger*," as opposed to a Communist sympathizer. Regardless, America started developing lists of people on whom to initiate investigations. If one wasn't an American, they were frequently targeted even more than the rest. Charlie Chaplin was "*blacklisted*" in 1947. The CIA, FBI and England worked jointly to gather material on Charlie Chaplin. Chaplin had been in all the gossip columns already due to his tumultuous relationship with Joan Barry, so the FBI, CIA and the MI5 – the secret British Intelligence agency collected files on Chaplin. They then spread the word in the media, especially the well-read publication, The Guardian, about his alleged Communistic ties after his movie, Monsieur Verdoux. Then the House Un-American Activities Committee (HUAC) apparently was deceived by a concocted story that Chaplin's birth name was "Israel Thornstein!"

❧

The year was 1953, when Charlie Chaplin and his wife at the time, Oona O'Neill, went to London to see the premiere of Limelight. They then visited South Africa for a brief vacation. In the meantime, the HUAC contacted MI5 for their investigations on Communists living in the Western countries. MI5 did so and reported,

> *"We have no trace in our records of this man, nor are we satisfied that there are any reliable grounds for regarding him as a security risk."*

That didn't satisfy J. Edgar Hoover, head of the FBI, and Charlie was denied a re-entry permit into the United States. Charlie was furious at this maltreatment and denied all the misrepresentations and negative propaganda he heard in the American media.

THE ESTATE

❦

C harlie and Oona then looked for property in Europe on which to settle. Together they found a beautiful manor house on a 35-acres estate in Switzerland. It was done in the Neo-Classic style and settled there. It was near the picturesque Lake Geneva. The Swiss Alps could be seen from his property.

❦

The name of the manor was Manoir de Ban. The property is well-treed and had a wine vineyard. The wine had originally been stored in the wine cellar which Chaplin used to provide a suitable humidity level for the preservation of his original films. Chaplin was very fond of spending his later years tending to a large vegetable garden.

❦

Oona O'Neill, who had the freedom to travel to the United States, flew back to America, closed his studio and transferred his finances to Europe. A year later, she renounced her American citizenship and became an English citizen.

THE CHAPLIN REVUE

❧

I n 1959, Charlie Chaplin was becoming feeble, so he
focused his efforts on refining and altering some of his
earlier works. One was The Chaplin Revue, combining
three of his silent shorties – A Dog's Life, The Pilgrim and
Shoulder Arms.

❧

In 1962, he received the honorary degree, Doctor of Letters,
from Oxford University at Durham. That is awarded to
people who have made significant contributions to the
humanities. He was also honored at the Cannes Film Festival
and the Venice Film Festival. The well-known theater critic,
Roger Ebert once related a story about spotting Charlie when
his movies were being shown on a giant screen in the city
square, Piazza San Marco. Ebert and the crowd cheered him,
shouting, *"Charlie! Charlie!"*

❦

In New York during the following year – 1963 – the Plaza Theater made arrangements to license the rights to some of his most notable movies like Limelight and Monsieur Verdoux. Chaplin was in attendance in a balcony seat.

THE "AMERICAN APOLOGY"

༄

The Academy of Motion Picture Arts and Sciences, founded in 1927, later became what is more popularly known as The Oscars. An Oscar is given to those for lifetime achievement in the motion picture industry. Douglas Fairbanks, whom Chaplin knew from his first stint in the business with First National Pictures, was the Academy's first president. In an unprecedented move, America invited him back in 1972 to Hollywood to receive that award and he came over. Commentators indicated that this gesture also represented a means by which the United States could apologize for his treatment during the McCarthy years.

༄

In 1980, the United States attorney-general announced that there was no evidence that Charlie Chaplin was a subversive and would be admitted back to the United States to live if he so wished. After the maltreatment he received, Chaplin said he was

"fed up with America's insults and moral pomposity,"

and didn't return after he received his Oscar.

SIR CHARLES SPENCER CHAPLIN

❦

Queen Elizabeth II, not to be outdone, knighted Charlie Chaplin in 1975. He was extremely frail at that time but was honored by that. This coincided with a documentary about his life called The Gentleman Tramp.

DEATH AND THE BODY
SNATCHERS

❧

Over the last ten years of his life, Chaplin had had a series of minor strokes. He was failing. On Christmas of the year 1977, he died in his sleep, reportedly of a massive stroke. He was 88-years-old.

❧

Just a year later, two immigrants disinterred his body and held it for ransom! They contacted Oona O'Neill, demanding $600,000. In addition, they threatened her children. The police monitored her telephone and sat in surveillance on the public phone booths in the immediate area. O'Neill also refused to pay the ransom. Several weeks later, the police arrested Gantscho Ganev and Roman Wardas, two unemployed auto mechanics. They confessed to the crime and pointed out a cornfield from which the body was recovered. Wardas was sentenced to four years of hard labor, but Ganev only got a suspended sentence. To prevent any further disruptions of his gravesite in Switzerland, the entire grave was recast in concrete along with that of Oona O'Neill who died in 1991.

❧ VII ❧
CONCLUSION

✿

Charlie Chaplin is a true *"rags-to-riches"* story, but he deserved all the recognition he received by the world who heralded him for his artistic accomplishments. He was a *"purist"* in the sense of being a perfectionist who carefully coordinated all the elements involved in the making of movies – the direction, production, the acting and even the music. Most writers of comedy have lived through very tragic events in their own lives, as Charlie Chaplin did, learned the art of managing to see events from a very wide perspective. In some ways, one might say he was the *"sad clown."* His expertise was in silent film in which he could show many of the aspects of daily life – frustrations, mishaps, mistaken identities and contradictions – all of which pepper daily life in the world today.

❧ VIII ☙
FURTHER READING

❦

- Carr, R. (2017) Charlie Chaplin: A Political Biography from Victorian Britain to Modern America. Taylor & Francis
- Kamin, D. (2008) The Comedy of Charlie Chaplin: Artistry in Motion. Scarecrow Press.
- Lynn, K. (1997) Charlie Chaplin and His Times. New York, NY: Simon & Schuster.

YOUR FREE EBOOK!

As a way of saying thank you for reading our book, we're offering you a free copy of the below eBook.

Happy Reading!